Is There a Conflict Between Science and Christianity?

Booklets in the Searching Issues series:

Is There a Conflict Between Science and Christianity?

NICKY GUMBEL

First published 1994
Revised edition 2013
This new edition 2016

10 09 08 07 06 05 04 03 02 01

ISBN: 978 1 909309 51 7

Published by Alpha International
HTB Brompton Road
London SW7 IJA
Email: publications@alpha.org
Website: alpha.org
@alphacourse

Illustrated by Charlie Mackesy

Contents

Is There A Conflict Between Science and Christianity?

The image often portrayed by the media, for whom any confrontation is news, is that Christian belief and science are in direct conflict. An article entitled 'God vs. Science' in *Time* magazine wrote about how some contemporary critics of religion are:

> Radicalized enough to publicly pick an ancient scab: the idea that science and religion, far from being complementary responses

> to the unknown, are at utter odds – or, as
> Yale psychologist Paul Bloom has written
> bluntly, 'Religion and science will always
> clash.' The market seems flooded with books
> by scientists describing a caged death match
> between science and God – with science
> winning, or at least chipping away at faith's
> underlying verities.[1]

Do 'religion and science always clash?' That is the question that this booklet seeks to explore.

First, there have certainly been periods in the history of Christianity when the church has opposed the results of scientific study. Galileo, the seventeenth-century Italian astronomer, found himself in conflict with the Roman Catholic Church over his discovery that planets revolve around the sun. He was tried by the inquisition in Rome, ordered to recant and spent the final eight years of his life under house arrest.

Persecution of scientists did not end in the seventeenth century. As late as 1925, John T. Scopes, a high-school teacher from Drayton, Tennessee, was prosecuted for violating the state law by teaching the theory of evolution. He was convicted and fined $100. On appeal, he was acquitted on the technicality that he had been fined excessively.

Second, it is thought by many that modern scientific study explains everything that was once explained by belief in God, so that such belief is now redundant. Further, it is argued that the assured results of modern science are in direct conflict with the teaching of the Bible. Some would say, for example, that modern science shows that miracles do not happen, whereas the Bible is full of miracles. Others claim that the scientific theory of the gradual evolution of humans and their organisms by natural processes is inconsistent with the account of creation in Genesis 1. The English biologist and agnostic philosopher T. H. Huxley (1825–95), for example, said, 'The doctrine of evolution, if consistently accepted, makes it impossible to believe the Bible.' Oxford scientist Richard Dawkins comes to a similar conclusion in a chapter on Darwinism, in which he concludes that 'God almost certainly does not exist'.[2]

In this booklet I want to look at how science and Christian belief relate to each other and, in particular, whether there is a conflict between 'the assured results of modern science' and the Christian faith.

Science and Christian faith are not incompatible

It was the Judeo-Christian worldview that provided the right environment for modern science to emerge. First, the Christian faith is monotheistic. Belief in one God led people to expect a uniformity in nature, with the underlying laws of nature remaining the same in time and space. A universe that was capricious and irregular would not be capable of systematic study.

Second, the Christian doctrine of creation by a rational God of order led scientists to expect a world that was both ordered and intelligible. Sixteenth-century scientists reasoned that the universe must be orderly and worthy of investigation because it was the work of an intelligent creator. 'Men became scientific because they expected Law in Nature, and they expected Law in Nature because they believed in a Legislator.'[3]

Third, the Christian belief in a transcendent God, separate from nature, meant that experimentation was justified. This would not have been the case under belief systems that regarded forms of matter as gods. Nor would it have been wise to experiment if you believed, as some did, that matter was essentially evil. The Christian worldview was that matter was good, but that was not God. So the Christian doctrine of creation 'provided an essential matrix for the coming into being of the scientific enterprise'.[4]

That Christian belief provided fertile soil for scientific experimentation is recognised by scientists, historians and philosophers. The British Oxford University physicist Dr Peter Hodgson writes, 'Christianity provided just those beliefs that are essential for science, and the whole moral climate that encouraged its growth.'[5] The historian Herbert Butterfield stated that 'science is a child of Christian thought'. The philosopher John MacMurray put it like this: 'Science is the legitimate child of a great religious movement, and its genealogy goes back to Jesus.'[6]

Some of the greatest scientists have been Christians

It is a well-established fact that for much of history Christianity and scientific study have been allies and not opponents.

Nicolaus Copernicus (1473–1543) laid the foundations of modern astronomy and the scientific revolution by suggesting, on mathematical grounds, that the earth travelled round the sun. He held office in the Roman Catholic Church in Poland as Canon of Frauenburg Cathedral and described God as 'the Best and Most Orderly Workman of all'.

Mathematician, physicist and astronomer Galileo Galilei (1564–1642) was the founder of modern mechanics and experimental physics. He argued that the earth was not the centre of the universe. Although he was persecuted by the church, he was a devout Roman Catholic Christian and once said, 'There are two big books, the book of nature and the book of supernature, the Bible.'

The founder of modern optics was the brilliant early astronomer and mathematician Johannes Kepler (1571–1630), best known for his discovery of the three principles of planetary motion. He was a deeply sincere Lutheran and said that he was 'thinking God's thoughts after Him.'

Perhaps the greatest scientist of all time was Sir Isaac Newton (1642–1727). He was certainly one of the most towering scientific intellects in history. He is well known for his formulation for the laws of gravity. He was also an expert in the field of optics, astronomy, differential calculus and responsible for the first correct analysis of white light. He believed in the inspiration of Scripture and wrote theological as well as scientific books, regarding his theological books as more important. He believed that no sciences were better attested than the religion of the Bible.

Michael Faraday (1791–1867) was one of the greatest scientists of the nineteenth century. He discovered the phenomenon of electromagnetic induction. He was the first to produce an electric current from a magnetic field. He invented the first electric motor and dynamo. Again, the Christian faith was the single most important influence upon him.

The same is true of many other pioneering scientists. Joseph Lister pioneered antiseptic surgery; Louis Pasteur originated pasteurisation; Gregor Mendel helped form the basis for the science of genetics; Lord Kelvin was a leading light in the foundation of modern physics; James Clerk Maxwell formulated electromagnetic theory. All these leading scientists were Christians.

Professor James Simpson, who paved the way for painless surgery through anaesthetics, was asked, 'What do you think is the most important discovery of your life?' He replied, 'The most important discovery I ever made was when I discovered Jesus Christ.'

In our own day there are a large number of scientists who are professing Christians. Christians in Science has over 1,000 members.[7] It would seem that numbers are not declining: 'In 1916, researchers asked biologists, physicists and mathematicians whether they believed in a God who actively communicates with humankind and to whom one may pray in expectation of receiving an answer. About 40 per cent answered in the affirmative.' Nearly 100 years later, in 1997, the same survey found that the percentage was almost identical. According to a 2009 study by the Pew

Research Center, just over 50 per cent of American scientists believe in a God, while 40 per cent do not.[8]

One of the leading scientists of our generation is Revd Dr John Polkinghorne KBE FRS, former Professor of Mathematical Physics and Dean and Chaplain of Trinity Hall, as well as former President of Queen's College, Cambridge. In 2002 he was awarded the prestigious Templeton Prize. He wrote:

> Men of religion can learn from science what the physical world is really like in its structure and long-evolving history. This constrains what religion can say where it speaks of that world as God's creation. He is clearly a patient God who works through process and not by magic. Men of science can receive from religion a deeper understanding than could be obtained from science alone. The physical world's deep mathematical intelligibility (signs of the Mind behind it) and finely tuned fruitfulness (expressive of divine purpose) are reflections of the fact that it is a creation.[9]

We could also note prominent contemporary figures such as Sir John Houghton FRS CBE, a leading UK scientist who was co-chair of the working group of the Intergovernmental Panel on Climate Change (IPCC) for fourteen years. In 2007, Houghton shared the Nobel Peace Prize with former US Vice-President Al Gore.

He was also Professor in Atmospheric Physics at the University of Oxford, former Chief Executive at the Met Office and he is a founder member of the International Society for Science and Religion.

Another example is Francis Collins, whose conversion to Christianity is described in the seventh booklet in this series: 'Is Faith Irrational?. As head of the Human Genome Project, he led a team of over 2,000 scientists who collaborated to determine the three billion letters of the human genome – our own DNA instruction book. It would take thirty-one years to read those letters aloud. This information is inside every single one of the 100 trillion cells in our bodies. Each genome contains enough information to fill a library of about 5,000 books. If all the chromosomes in a single body were laid out end to end, they would stretch 100 billion miles. Our brains alone have a billion nerve cells. As the steward of the study of this great mystery, Collins speaks of 'a richly satisfying harmony between the scientific and the spiritual worldviews'. He also said, 'I am a scientist and a believer, and I find no conflict between those world views.'[10]

Science and Scripture do not contradict each other

It is probably true that there are more disagreements and apparent contradictions within science itself than between science and the Christian faith. Nevertheless, it is commonly thought that there are conflicts between science and theology.

One of the alleged conflicts is in the area of miracles.[11] Spinoza (1632–77), the Dutch Jewish philosopher and the foremost exponent of seventeenth-century rationalism, declared that nothing can 'contravene nature's universal laws'. He believed in a mechanistic uniformity of nature. The philosopher David Hume defined a miracle as 'a violation of the laws of nature'.[12] Consequently, he rejected miracles, suggesting they are impossible. However, this is a circular argument. If the laws of nature are defined as completely uniform, then the supernatural is ruled out from the start and it is therefore impossible to believe in miracles, however strong the evidence.

Yet many have pointed to this conflict between the Bible and science. In 1937, the distinguished German physicist Max Planck said, 'Faith in miracles must yield ground, step by step, before the steady and firm advance of the forces of science, and its total defeat is indubitably a mere matter of time.'[13] Planck implied that science now explains what was once thought to be miraculous, which suggests that those who believed in miracles in the past did so because they didn't sufficiently understand the laws of nature. This is not the case. In Jesus' day everyone knew, just as well as we do, that, for example, it is not 'natural' for a virgin to have a baby or for someone to rise from the dead. If they had had no knowledge of the laws of nature, then they would not have recognised a miracle in any shape or form. As the famed novelist and English professor C. S. Lewis said, 'Belief in miracles, far from depending on an ignorance of the laws of nature, is only possible in so far as those laws are known.'[14]

The real issue is, 'Is there a God?' If there is, then miracles become a real possibility. If God is God, then he created matter, reason, time, space and all scientific laws, and therefore is at liberty to interfere. If there is no God, then miracles are a problem. But philosophy and science alone will not answer the crucial question. Scientific laws are not laws like the laws of pure mathematics, which cannot be broken. Rather, they are descriptive. As John Stott put it, 'I am not suggesting that miracles are an adequate basis for theism. But, once we have come on other grounds to believe in God... it becomes logical to affirm, and illogical to deny, the possibility of the miraculous. For "natural laws" describe God's activity; they do not control it.'[15]

Is there a conflict between creation and evolution?

The second area of alleged conflict is the theory of evolution and the biblical account of creation. Is there an irreconcilable conflict?

The first point to note is that much of the theory of evolution is still only theory. It is necessary to distinguish between micro- and macro-evolution. Micro-evolution (which could not conceivably be said to conflict with the Bible) means the variation and development within a species. The horse, for example, has increased greatly in size and developed in other ways over time. This kind of evolution has been observed and there is overwhelming evidence for it.

Macro-evolution, on the other hand, means evolution from one species to another – the most famous example being from apes to humans. It is often thought of as fact but is still unproved and remains a theory that is not accepted by all scientists.[16] It is important to stress the provisionality of all scientific theories. The most striking example in modern times is Newtonian physics, which was treated with the utmost respect and regarded as virtually incontestable until Einstein and others showed that its laws broke down for the very, very small (where quantum mechanics becomes relevant) and the very, very fast (where relativity becomes relevant). Particular versions of theories of evolution are still taught in schools as if they are the aforementioned 'assured results of modern science'. To regard a scientific theory as more than provisional is bad science.

The second important point is that there are many different interpretations of Genesis held by sincere

Christians. Some believe in a literal six-day creation. The Creation Research Society, formed in 1963 as a committee of ten scientists in Michigan, USA, whose membership is limited to scientists having at least a graduate degree in a natural or applied science, now has hundreds of members. They believe that all types of living things were made by direct acts of God during the creation week. Whatever biological changes have occurred since then have been only within the original created kinds.

Other Christians interpret Genesis 1 differently. They point out that the Hebrew word for 'day' (*yom*) has many different meanings, even within Scripture. Since the sun did not appear until day four, the writer probably did not mean 24-hour days. The word *yom* can mean a long period of time. When read in this way, it is not in conflict with the prevailing scientific view of the vast age of the universe, nor is it in conflict with a gradual evolution in which God not only started the process, but worked within it to produce a system that culminated in human life. They point out that the chronological order of Genesis 1 begins with plants, then animals, and finally humans, in perhaps a similar way to that now accepted by evolutionary theorists.

Some add the suggestion that Genesis is about information fed in at intervals ('And God said...'). The feeding in of information takes place in a short period of time. The working out of that information takes much longer. They point out that this corresponds remarkably with the theory of the Big Bang, where the essential things happened within the first few minutes.

Many Christians read Genesis 1 as poetic in form, which is not necessarily connected with chronological events in history. It is a pre-scientific and non-scientific account of creation, dealing with matters outside the scope of science. Poetic language can be true without being literally true. When the psalmist wrote, 'The world is firmly established; it cannot be moved' (Psalm 93:1), he was using a poetic image. But Galileo's opponents took it literally and argued that the earth was stationary and that theories of the earth orbiting the sun were wrong. These Christians feel that, in the same way, the early chapters of Genesis should not be taken literally. They say that there is strong evidence for macro-evolutionary theory and that it is now accepted by the vast majority of scientists who argue that the fossil evidence is inconsistent with a literal interpretation of the Genesis account. Those who take this view argue that what matters is that it is God who created and sustains the laws of physics and nature that evolved over time, culminating in human life.

Whichever view one takes, it is clear that there is not necessarily a conflict between science and Scripture. In the light of the uncertainty and the difference of opinions among genuine Christians, I think it is unwise to be too dogmatic about the issue (certainly if, like me, you are neither a scientist nor a theologian).

The main point of Genesis 1 is not to answer the questions 'How?' and 'When?' (the scientific questions), but the questions 'Why?' and 'Who?' (the theological questions). The Bible is not primarily a scientific book, but a theological one. It offers a personal explanation more than a scientific one. The scientific explanation does not prove or disprove the personal one. Rather it is complementary. Even Stephen Hawking, arguably the most brilliant scientist of his generation, has admitted that 'science may solve the problem of how the universe began, but it cannot answer the question: why does the universe bother to exist?'[17]

Dr John Lennox uses the following illustration:

> Suppose I wheel in the most magnificent cake ever seen and I had in front of me various fellows of every academic and learned society in the world and I picked the top men and I tell tem to analyse the cake for me. So out steps the world famous nutritionist and he talks about the balance of the various foods that form this cake. Then a leading biochemist analyses the cake at the bio-chemical level. Then a chemist says, 'Well, yes of course, but now we must get down to the very basic chemicals that form this.' Then the physicist comes on and says, 'Well, yes, these people

have told you something, but you really need to get down to the electrons and the protons and the quarks.' And last of all the stage is occupied by the mathematician. And he says, 'Ultimately you need to understand the fundamental equations governing the motion of all the electrons and protons in this cake.' And they finish and it is a magnificent analysis of the cake. And then I turn round to them and I say, 'Ladies and Gentlemen, I've just got one more question for you. Tell me why the cake was made. And there in front of them stands Aunt Mathilda who made the cake. It's only when the person who made the cake is prepared to disclose why she's made it that they'll ever understand why. No amount of scientific analysis, however exhaustive and detailed, can answer that question. And then Aunt Mathilda in the end says, 'I'll let you out of your misery. I've made the cake for my nephew Johnny – it's his birthday next week.'

Dr John Lennox affirms that 'No amount of scientific analysis of this planet on which we stand will tell you why it was made unless the Creator chooses himself to speak. The fantastic thing is that he has spoken and what he has spoken is called Genesis.' There is therefore no necessary conflict between evolution, which attempts to describe the mechanism of creation, and Genesis, which describes the meaning of creation.

Science and Scripture complement each other

God has revealed himself both in creation and supremely in Jesus Christ, as witnessed to in the Scriptures. Science is the study of God's general revelation in creation. Biblical theology is the study of God's 'special' revelation in Jesus and the Scriptures.

The psalmist speaks of this general revelation in the natural world:

> The heavens declare the glory of God; the skies proclaim the work of his hands. Day after day they pour forth speech; night after night they display knowledge. There is no speech or language where their voice is not heard. Their voice goes out into all the earth, their words to the ends of the world.
> Psalm 19:1–4a

The apostle Paul makes a similar claim: 'For since the creation of the world God's invisible qualities – his eternal power and divine nature – have been understood from what has been made, so that they are without excuse' (Romans 1:20; see also Acts 14:17; 17:22–28).

Some have argued, as William Paley did in the eighteenth century, that the existence of God could be proved from 'natural theology', ie, God's general revelation in creation. Perhaps that is going too far. What can be said is that God the Creator has made a world in which there is much to suggest the presence of 'more than meets the eye', and he has not left it wholly without marks of his character.

There are two main arguments for this. First, there is the argument that since everything has a cause there must be a first cause. The popular version of this is in the story of the Hyde Park orator in London who was attacking belief in God. He argued that the world just happened. As he spoke, a soft tomato was thrown at him. 'Who threw that?' he demanded angrily. A voice from the back of the crowd replied, 'No one threw it – it threw itself.'

This argument is not a proof, but it is a pointer. It is easier to believe that God created something out of nothing than to believe that nothing created something out of nothing. Towards the end of his life, Charles Darwin wrote of

> the impossibility of conceiving this immense
> and wonderful universe including man as a
> result of blind chance or necessity. When

> thus reflecting, I feel compelled to look to a
> first cause having an intelligent mind in some
> degree analogous to that of man and I deserve
> to be called a theist.[18]

The second argument is based on the evidence of design. Again, this does not amount to a 'proof', but is a powerful indicator.

Professor Chandra Wickramasinghe, who comes from a Buddhist background, has said, 'The chances that life just occurred on earth are about as unlikely as a typhoon blowing through a junkyard and constructing a Boeing 747.'[19]

The matter of design has recently come to the fore with the 'anthropic principle'. The physical constraints of nature are so finely tuned that, if they were slightly different, we would not exist.

> In the early expansion of the universe there has
> to be a close balance between the expansive
> energy (driving things apart) and the force of
> gravity (pulling things together). If expansion
> dominated then matter would fly apart too
> rapidly for condensation into galaxies and
> stars to take place. Nothing interesting could
> happen in so thinly spread a world. On the
> other hand, if gravity dominated the world
> would collapse in on itself again before

there was time for the processes of life to get going. For us to be possible requires a balance between the effects of expansion and contraction which at a very early epoch in the universe's history (the Planck time) has to differ from equality by not more than 1 in 10^{60}. The numerate will marvel at such a degree of accuracy. For the non-numerate I will borrow an illustration from Paul Davies[20] of what that accuracy means. He points out that it is the same as aiming at a target an inch wide on the other side of the observable universe, twenty thousand million light years away, and hitting the mark![21]

Stephen Hawking makes the point that,

If the density of the universe one second after the Big Bang had been greater by one part in a thousand billion, the universe would have recollapsed after ten years. On the other hand, if the density of the universe at that time had been less by the same amount, the universe would have been essentially empty since it was about ten years old. How was it that the initial density of the universe was chosen so carefully? Maybe there is some reason why the universe should have precisely the critical density?[22]

Although he does not believe in a creator God, his own theory would seem to point in that direction.

Nor is it just life that has to be explained. It is intelligent life, the human mind, the rational structure of the world, beauty, human love, friendship and justice. These are all dimensions of reality that point beyond chemical and biological laws. Could all this simply be the result of blind chance and natural selection, with no intelligent mind behind the process?

The evidence of science may point to the existence of God. General revelation suggests the tremendous power, intelligence and imagination of a personal creator. But without the special revelation of Jesus Christ as witnessed to in the Scriptures, we would have known little about him.

Albert Einstein, writing from a Jewish perspective, said, 'A legitimate conflict between science and religion cannot exist. Science without religion is lame; religion without science is blind.' Science without religion is lame for a number of reasons. First, we cannot find the God of the Bible through science alone. 'Unfortunately for the scientifically minded, God is not discoverable or demonstrable by purely scientific means. But that really proves nothing; it simply means that the wrong instruments are being used for the job.'[23] We need God's special revelation as well as his general revelation. The first six verses of Psalm 19 speak of God's general revelation. The next verses speak of God's special revelation through his law. It is only through his special revelation that we can find 'the God and Father of our Lord Jesus Christ'.

Second, science cannot speak to the deepest needs of men and women. Lewis Wolpert writing in *The Times* said, 'Scientists, or anyone else, without religion, have to face a world in which there is no real purpose, no meaning to torment and joy, and accept that when we are dead we vanish, that there is no after-life.'[24] Science has nothing to say to these deep levels of human experience. It cannot deal with the problem of loneliness or hearts broken by grief. Science is unable to solve the moral dilemmas of humankind. It has no remedy for the problem of unforgiven sin and guilt. Only in the cross of Christ do we find the answer to these problems.

Bestselling novelist Susan Howatch had houses in several countries and drove a Porsche and a Mercedes. She said that, after the break-up of her marriage, 'God seized me by the scruff of the neck' and she became a Christian. Recently, she gave £1 million to Cambridge University to finance a lectureship in theology and natural science, having come to the conclusion that science and theology were 'two aspects of the truth'. We need science and scientists. Our civilisation owes a great deal to their work. But more than that we need Christianity and we need Jesus Christ.

Endnotes

1. *Time*, 'God vs. Science', 5 November 2006.
2. Richard Dawkins, *The God Delusion*, (Black Swan, 2006), p.189.
3. C. S. Lewis, *Miracles* (Collins, C. S. Lewis Signature Classics Edition, 2012) p.169.
4. John Polkinghorne, *One World* (SPCK, 1986), p.1.
5. Cited in William Oddie (ed.), *After the Deluge* (SPCK, 1987), p.118.
6. John MacMurray, *Reason and Emotion* (Faber, 1961), p.172.
7. cis.org.uk/about-cis
8. articles.latimes.com/2009/nov/24/opinion/la-oe-masci24-2009nov24
9. John Polkinghorne, *The Daily Telegraph*, 24 August 1992.
10. CNN, 'Collins: Why this scientist believes in God', 6 April 2007, edition.cnn.com/2007/US/04/03/collins.commentary/index.html
11. The term 'miracle' is sometimes used very loosely to describe, for example, remarkable answers to prayer. It is helpful to distinguish 'providence', ie, the guiding or steering by God of nature, humankind and history, from a 'miracle', which has been well-defined by David Atkinson (*The Wings of Refuge*, IVP, 1983, p.13) as a 'non-repeatable, counter-instance of an otherwise demonstrable law of nature', eg, walking on water, raising the dead or multiplying food.
12. David Hume, *On Miracles* (1748), p.114.
13. Max Planck, *Scientific Autobiography* (Williams and Norgate, 1950), p.155.
14. C. S. Lewis, *op cit*, p.75.
15. John Stott, *Essentials* (Hodder & Stoughton, 1988), p.221.
16. Dr James Moore has pointed out that, contrary to popular belief, it was not the theologians who opposed Darwin as much as the scientists. 'It was few theologians and many scientists who dismissed Darwinism and evolution' (Michael Poole, *Science and*

Belief, Lion, 1990, p.102).

17. Stephen Hawking, *Black Holes and Baby Universes and Other Essays* (Bantam Press, 1993).

18. Charles Darwin, cited in Francis S. Collins, *The Language of God: A Scientist Presents Evidence for Belief* (Simon & Schuster, 2007), p.99.

19. In 'Threats on Life of Controversial Astronomer', *New Scientist*, 21 January 1982, p.140, quoted in Dean L. Overman, *A Case Against Accident and Self-Organization* (Rowman & Littlefield Publishers, Inc., 2001).

20. British physicist Paul Davies, author of *God and the New Physics* and other works, is one of the most popular science writers today. He is notably unsympathetic to conventional Christianity.

21. John Polkinghorne, *One World* (SPCK, 1986), p.57.

22. Stephen Hawking, *op cit*.

23. J.B. Phillips, *Gathered Gold* (Evangelical Press, 1984).

24. *The Times*, 10 April 1993.

Further Reading

Francis Collins, *The Language of God: A Scientist Presents Evidence for Belief* (Pocket Books, 2007)

Roger Forster and Paul Marston, *Reason and Faith* (Monarch, 1989)

Alister McGrath, *Surprised by Meaning: Science, Faith and How We Make Sense of Things* (Westminster/John Knox Press, 2011)

John Polkinghorne, *One World* (SPCK, 1986)

Alpha

Alpha is a practical introduction to the Christian faith, initiated by HTB in London and now being run by thousands of churches, of many denominations, throughout the world. If you are interested in finding out more about the Christian faith and would like details of your nearest Alpha, please visit our website:

alpha.org

or contact:
The Alpha Office,
HTB Brompton Road,
London,
SW7 1JA

Tel: 0845 644 7544